RAMEN NOODLE RESUME

Ramen Noodle Resume © 2020 by Chris Komisarjevsky.

First edition published 2020

Printed in the United States of America

ISBN (paperback): 978-1-7346415-0-9
ISBN (ebook): 978-1-7346415-1-6

Cover and Interior Design by Alexia Garaventa

Library of Congress Cataloging-in-Publication Data

To those determined to find the right job

In the spirit of the optimist to whom every difficulty is an opportunity, and not as the pessimist, to whom every opportunity presents some difficulty.

—Bertram Carr, mayor of Carlisle, England, 1919

In a digital world, how to write a resume for the job you want
… before college graduation comes around and those ramen noodles run out

RAMEN NOODLE RESUME

CHRIS KOMISARJEVSKY
With a Foreword by RONI AVISSAR, PhD

With appreciation to

My wife, Reina, and our nine children, who read the manuscript to "keep it real."

Dean Roni Avissar, Justin Fox, Julie Biber and Pat Ford, who generously shared their thoughts and experience.

Alexia Garaventa, whose design of the book made it grab attention from cover to cover and whose intuition captured the concept perfectly.

Katie Haigler, whose proofreading made the ideas and words flow.

And to all those who listened to my guidance about their resumes and landed great jobs
… I'm sure I learned more than they did.

THANK YOU.

TABLE OF CONTENTS

PREFACE

YOU'RE ON YOUR WAY

You deserve the best chance for getting a job you want

You've worked hard in college and are on the cusp of an exciting journey toward a career. You deserve every chance to get the job you want. You shouldn't have to settle for the first one that comes around.

While this book outlines steps to help you get there, the process is far from simple. The best jobs are competitive, and landing one means that you must not only showcase your skills and potential but also communicate your passion and how you can add value to a company.

Think of it this way. For a successful job search, there must be a meeting of the minds when it comes to goals and expectations both for the employer and for the candidate—that's you.

For the employer, the goal is to identify and hire someone with talent, skills, some experience, high energy and potential. The expectation is that the candidate will become an employee who will work hard, mature professionally, eagerly accept challenges and become an ever-more productive member of the team, helping to make the organization successful.

For you, the goal is to land the kind of job that will be exciting and intellectually challenging, a role you can be passionate about and one in which you can make a meaningful contribution. Above all, your expectation is to work hard, with the belief that this first job is a critical step toward a career where you can grow and be rewarded fairly.

I know this firsthand. As a retired chief executive of a worldwide public relations counseling firm, I have been responsible for hiring talented staff, and have watched how great hires fulfilled our mission, expanded our reputation and helped us reach our financial goals. On the other side, as a father of nine and a mentor for many college students and grads, I've learned lessons along the way that can make all the difference between landing a rewarding job and struggling with a job that just doesn't seem to fit.

This book is for rising college seniors, their parents and all those higher education career counselors whose mandate is to help graduating college students focus on the search for a career and landing that job.

This book started as notes I took while working with rising seniors and grads on their job applications. Invariably, the discussions turned to how hard it was to write a resume that was impactful—and short and to the point.

In addition to my own experiences, I drew on two other sources to write this book: The first was *How Not to Write* by celebrated Pulitzer Prize winner and widely read and respected columnist William Safire, which tells readers the correct way to write, and when it's all right to break the rules. The second source was advertising guru David Ogilvy, author of *Confessions of an Advertising Man*, whose advice is as valid for today's world of social media and digital communications as it was decades ago:

- Write the way you talk. Naturally.

- Use short words, short sentences and short paragraphs.

- Never use jargon words.

- Never write more than two pages on any subject.

I hope this book proves to be a motivating and easy read and helps you find a great job.

With best wishes for a great career,

Chris

———————————————————**//**———————————————————

For a successful job search, there must be a meeting of the minds ...

FOREWORD

THE VERY BEST JOB POSSIBLE

DEAN RONI AVISSAR, PhD

Rosenstiel School of Marine and Atmospheric Science,
University of Miami

Success for an institution of higher learning is measured in great part by the quality of its faculty and the contributions that will be made by its students after they graduate and go on to build their careers.

Together, they speak to a college or university's reputation for excellence and the vital role that all of us—whether faculty or staff—have in training those who will go on to improve our world through research, business, education or public service.

From a practical perspective, when we do that well, we have a leg up in attracting the best professors, ensuring our legacy through a growing student body and making it possible for us to have a robust development initiative, which, in turn, provides the funding for scholarships, new study programs, research facilities and campus expansion.

I believe then that it is one of our responsibilities to help coach those soon-to-be graduates as they begin their job search.

Why? It is the natural extension of our mission.

At the University of Miami, our mission is "to transform lives through education, research, innovation, and service." At the Rosenstiel School of Marine and Atmospheric Science, we take that one step further through our focus on cutting-edge scientific research "to transfer the knowledge gained to our students, the national and scientific community, and to policymakers and the public."

We know full well that research and hypotheses are just the beginning of an exploration into what happens or needs to happen. The long-term goal is to be able to understand and put into action the practical application of what was explored in the ocean, researched in the lab or studied in the classroom.

Making theory practical is why the Rosenstiel School chose to invest and build the largest wind-wave simulator in the world to study the interaction of the winds, waves, ocean currents and storm surges under simulated hurricane conditions and make the findings practical. It is why we have a ninety-six-foot catamaran research vessel, the *F.G. Walton Smith*, to explore shallow-water mangroves and reefs and provide a unique kind of training that proves valuable both during studies and after graduation. It is why we bring our students to the Galapagos to give them hands-on experience researching the impact that volcanoes have on the atmosphere, marine life and the environment. And it is why we are redefining the paradigm in undergraduate STEM education by immersing our students as a team into real, cutting-edge research projects.

As I see it, this is science made practical. Using knowledge gained during undergraduate and graduate studies, we prepare our graduates so that they can be productive and are able to transform lives, influence policy, innovate for business and take new approaches to environmental challenges.

This is a very clear mandate for all of us at the Rosenstiel School. We want strong ties with our graduates. They value their education, and we value them. They put what they have studied to work. They join an influential network for building career relationships.

As proud graduates, they are also a key element of our fundraising, since they often have the earning potential and capacity to give.

While education is the primary goal of universities, working with and encouraging rising seniors and grad students on their job search is an integral component of both student and university success.

In short, we want them to get the very best job possible.

———————————— **"** ————————————

... it is one of our responsibilities to help coach those soon-to-be graduates as they begin their job search.

1

YOUR RESUME IN THE DIGITAL WORLD

Strong and well written, it's still crucial

There are few college seniors or parents who don't get nervous when senior year rolls around and there are no job prospects on the horizon. Some might even gasp and feel a touch of panic when thoughts dwell too long on college loan payments coming due and images appear of college students moving into the basement, hanging out dorm-room-style at home.

All that tuition, the agony of term papers and the pressure to maintain a high GPA, along with countless packages of ramen noodles late at night, and now what?

Nothing new, some would say. We've seen this kind of pressure for a very long time. And while it's certainly true that the internet and all things digital have had a significant impact on the job search process—particularly on the way that jobs are posted, opportunities are shared and applications are submitted—the role of the resume remains supreme.

The online world has added job-hunting challenges by making it appear easier for applicants to really stand out. But that's not always the case. Social media has given too many young people the wrong impression that they have it made and are today's influencers because of the number of views, likes and followers they have or the approval they receive online from so-called friends. Social media stardom can be fleeting. And it may well turn out to be a double-edged sword, depending on what's being posted, since texts and photos live forever online. Either way, it's a rare case when social media fame proves to be the driving force behind landing that job.

Don't be under the impression that an active social media presence is the key to a job. If, when faced with preparing your resume, your first impulse is to fill that blank sheet of paper with your online posts—resist. They likely have little to do with the job you are applying for, and may detract from the perception of your abilities and potential.

There are other disappointments that technology has created for online job applicants. Your resume might never even be seen if it doesn't stand out with *key words*. Artificial intelligence and algorithms may skip over applications that don't appear to embody the exact qualifications being looked for. And you may never even know what happened to your application. If lucky, you might receive a canned "thank you for applying ... we will be in touch if your qualifications meet our needs" response. Experience will tell you that many online applicants never hear anything back even when they have applied to fifty or more different jobs.

What we do know is that in spite of all the changes brought about by the digital revolution, resumes are a vital tool that remains crucial to earning that job offer.

If your resume is not well thought out and does not demonstrate clear purpose, you'll be left behind. A poorly written resume might undermine your best efforts to get a job. Or if, like too many, your resume is just a hasty chronological list of companies, schools and dates, it will fall flat and add nothing to your application. And that would be a shame.

A powerful resume tells a compelling story about career goals, hard work and skills; illustrates a passion for learning; showcases successes at other jobs; and shares why your accomplishments are meaningful.

Your resume should take the reader on a journey that highlights your abilities and potential and gives insights into what makes you special.

Above all, a good resume gives you the opportunity to aim for the best and land the job you want. It is your career, and each step along the way—including this one right out of college—is an important building block for your future.

---***---

… it's a rare case when social media fame proves to be the driving force behind landing that job.

2

THAT ONE-PAGER IS YOUR SOURCE DOCUMENT

Every "upload" and "autofill" relies on it

You'd think things have changed since technology has pervaded every moment in our lives. But they haven't. Snapchat, Instagram, Facebook and all those contacts, followers, friends and likes don't substitute for a strong resume, a targeted job search and taking full advantage of job-search technology.

Your resume is alive and kicking, and it's as important as ever—possibly even more so. The ever-expanding array of social media hasn't killed it off. While technology and the digital world have certainly made so many other ways of communicating and reaching out possible, you still have to have that one page that shares your story.

While it may never even be printed, handed over in an interview or sealed in an envelope, your resume is core to your job search and your career. You will post it, extract from it and send it. You will constantly refer to it because it will be the guide for how you position yourself and sell your story.

After all, job search and hiring are two sides of the same coin. On one hand, you want to work and be part of an organization, and on the other, your employer wants to have someone work and be part of their organization. It's like any transaction: there's a seller and a buyer. And both must understand what they are getting and come to an agreement.

The first stage of that transaction begins with a single page—your resume.

It is on that page that you will gather your thoughts and write the words that will shape your job search.

Pivotal to your job search, your resume is your source document for all those online applications. You will turn to it right from the get-go when you are asked to *upload* your resume. Algorithms will extract background information, education credentials and employment history from it, and digital filters will sift through your work experience, academic history and extracurricular activities to see if you're the right *fit* for the job.

In fact, you can't even complete an online application without a resume that is available digitally.

Beyond those demands from technology, your resume is crucial because it provides structure, consistency and a clear statement about yourself and your goals. You need that kind of discipline. You will fill out countless applications before you land the perfect job.

And, without a good resume to pull from, the task will become overwhelming.

So, get started with that blank sheet of paper. Think hard before you start to write. Put a lot of thought into it. Otherwise, it's not going to be the most thoughtful picture of you, your accomplishments and your career aspirations.

Like most things in life worth doing, work hard at it.

Remember: getting a job is now your single most important job.

---------------------------**II**-----------------------------

While it may never even be printed, handed over in an interview or sealed in an envelope, your resume is core to your job search and your career.

3

JOB SEARCH IS TOUGH AND COMPETITIVE

You need to present more than just your degree to land that job

You and I would like to think that simply having a bachelor's degree and being educated would be the ticket to a great job.

Doesn't every business put a high priority on attracting young employees who bring smarts and skills?

Of course they do; but it takes more than that to land the job you want.

Just think about all of the millennials who've flooded the job market, bringing their own set of skills and strengths and looking at things differently than those who came before … and already having a significant impact on business and society.

How do you stand out from the others and get that job when the competition is so fierce?

Look at it this way: Each year, the independent and nonpartisan Institute of Education Sciences—the statistics, research and evaluation arm of the US Department of Education—publishes information on enrollment at American colleges and universities. The data are impressive when looking at the number of people attending colleges and universities and the number receiving degrees:

- Total enrollment each year in American colleges and universities is expected to reach 20.5 million students by 2027.

- Of that number, just shy of 4 million will be awarded degrees each year. With 19.9 million students currently enrolled, the expectation is that colleges and universities will award 1 million associate's degrees, 1.9 million bachelor's degrees, 780,000 master's degrees and 182,000 doctorates this year.[1]

Needless to say, the competition is significant. You're not alone in your talents, education or accomplishments.

Even in the best of years, when monthly employment is high and the economy strong, it takes work to put yourself at the head of the line, especially for the job you really want.

The bottom line is that getting that offer right out of college is not a slam dunk.

———————————————————*II*———————————————————

... competition is significant. You're not alone in your talents, education or accomplishments.

———————————————————————————————————————

1 Source: Institute of Education Sciences, "Back to School Statistics," National Center for Education Statistics, 2019, https://nces.ed.gov/fastfacts/display.asp?id=372.

4

OF COURSE, OTHER FACTORS HELP OPEN THE DOOR

Give yourself every advantage

Everyone who has ever searched for a job knows to pay close attention to a number of other factors that will give you an edge—but that edge won't necessarily get you the job.

Smart job applicants try to get on the inside track by finding the right connection to the right introduction at the right time to the right person.

They also take into account the role that artificial intelligence has come to play in the job search process. Technology has changed the game, especially when it comes to the importance of selecting the best words for your resume. Like it or not, digital programs are often the first reviewers of resumes sent electronically to human resource departments and employment agencies. If the job specs ask for certain qualifications, then your resume needs to use the same language or your application will go nowhere. Even when a human conducts the first review of your resume, those words still need to jump out, especially given how little time a reviewer will spend on each resume.

As you plan your resume, keep in mind that there are four other factors that will have an impact on your job search. They won't guarantee you the job, but they could well be the critical factor in landing that first interview:

Relationships, networking and internal recommendations: This is at the top of the list. Relationships are incredibly important for getting your foot in the door. Most companies conducting a search will pay closer attention to a candidate recommended by a respected source or one of their own employees. In fact, some companies provide bonuses to employees who recommend new hires.

Post-graduate education or specialized training: Jobs in science, technology, engineering and mathematics (STEM) and medicine and teaching require additional studies. That could take the form of a post-graduate degree, being part of a research program or attending specialized skill training. Those with advanced degrees or certifications will often be put at the head of the list of candidates.

Social media: Judiciously used, social media can be an effective tool. Blogs, thoughtful participation in podcasts and recognition from others can be assets. Overused or misused, however, social media will be a detriment. Internet stardom is often just a flash in the pan that doesn't last—and depending on your social media content, it can backfire.

Good timing: Don't discount being in the right place at the right time. You can't plan for it, but it does happen. When you see an opportunity, be ready to go for it.

---**II**---

… take into account the role that artificial intelligence has come to play in the job search process.

5

THE RESUME FORMAT IS A POWERFUL ORGANIZING TOOL

But words are the top priority and the first challenge

Smart use of formatting is a very important tool to organize your thoughts and draw the reader's attention to those qualities and skills that you want to stand out. A good format provides your thinking and background in an efficient and well-structured style that's easy to read and entices the reader to want more.

A direct, hard-hitting and upfront resume has impact.

Formats are pretty easy to find. You can get them online or in Microsoft Word. Often your friends and classmates will suggest theirs. Your college or university career counselor will also be able to show you some. And you can always format your own.

As an organizing tool, a resume format pushes you to provide the information and thinking that every recruiter expects to learn about: in particular, the details of your background education and work history, along with insights into your career goals. In fact, if you don't provide them in an easy-to-read format, you will be at a disadvantage. Even more to the point, you run the risk of a recruiter or prospective employer looking at your resume and wondering if you have purposely left things out for some unknown reason. That alone creates skepticism about your candidacy and raises more questions than answers.

The resume format gives you the chance to provide key details and, thereby, establish credibility.

At the very least, the format will urge you to provide the following:

- Current contact information
- Career objective, goal or personal statement
- Skills
- Areas of excellence
- Special experience
- Education history with school name, degree earned, GPA and dates
- Work history with an emphasis on accomplishments
- Specific employment experience and skills

However, the words you use are far more important and say much more about you, your career goals and your skills than a particular format.

Remember, what your resume *says* is the crucial challenge. Those words must describe you and provide a potential employer with a picture of what you will bring as an employee. They shape how a prospective employer evaluates your experience and skills. And they must give some specifics as to your accomplishments so employers can start to visualize what you can do for them and how you can have an impact in their organization.

So at the outset, just pick something simple that works for you. You'll likely change it anyway, especially after you have put in the time and energy needed to be introspective and carefully think through what you want your resume to say about you, your strengths, your experience and what makes you stand out.

―――――――――――――― // ――――――――――――――

The words you use are far more important and say much more about you, your career goals and your skills than a particular format.

6

DON'T DELAY

Getting started is the hardest part

Have you ever heard the apocryphal story about Napoleon Bonaparte and the construction of the Arc de Triomphe?

Well, it goes like this: In 1806, General Bonaparte commissioned the construction of the Arc de Triomphe in Paris as a monument and rallying point to celebrate French military victories. Even though it was not completed until well after his exile and subsequent death, the story continues that, during construction, one of Bonaparte's generals lamented that there were no shade trees to protect parading troops from the heat of the summer sun. Turning to Bonaparte, worried that his troops would be sweltering in the summer heat, in danger of exhaustion and risking collapse, he complained. Bonaparte looked at his general and simply said, "Well, you'd better get planting."

Now fast-forward to today.

As you get ready to start writing your resume and are staring at a blank sheet of paper, it's okay to feel overwhelmed and daunted by the task.

For many of you, you'll overcome those feelings and begin to write. With time, you'll focus on a career direction and landing that full-time job starts to feel like a strong possibility.

For some, though, staring at that piece of paper might help you focus on other opportunities, especially if you're not sure what direction you want your career to take. You might think about going on to graduate school, becoming an apprentice to learn a practical skill, taking specialized courses to earn a certification or forging an entrepreneurial path. Or you could decide that public service was in the cards, or that military service could give you certain skills and leadership experience that you desire.

Yes, all of those are options and can create a meaningful career path.

But if a full-time job is your goal, you need to put pen to paper or fingers to the keyboard and get that resume started early. Getting started is the toughest part.

If you doubt you can get those words down, read some of the writings of Antoine de Saint-Exupéry—the legendary French aviator and author most famous for writing *The Little Prince*—who started his career in 1926 as a pilot flying solo across the Mediterranean to carry mail from France to French West Africa. In his book *Wind, Sand and Stars*, he tells the story of the night before his very first flight: "I felt very meek. I felt myself ill-prepared." His friend and fellow pilot Guillaumet said to him, "You'll be bothered from time to time by storms, fog, snow. When you are, think of those who went through it before you, and say to yourself: 'What they can do, I can do.'"

So don't waste time. Start writing.

---**II**---

… if a full-time job is your goal, you need to put pen to paper or fingers to the keyboard and get that resume started early.

7

YOUR SPECIAL QUALITIES HELP DEFINE YOU

Showcase yourself

The goal of a resume is to showcase yourself to others. Not as an ego trip. Not to be boisterous. But to portray yourself as confident in a style that lets the reader learn how you tackle challenges, live your passions, follow your interests and fulfill your dreams.

After all, most students don't have much employment experience before graduation day. As a result, to be realistic, prospective employers of college grads focus more on an applicant's potential. Often, this means they look to a track record of summer jobs, internships and volunteer work as important clues about a candidate's determination, interests, life skills and work ethic.

Of course, no recruiter can read your mind or be expected to fill in the blanks. They've likely never met or heard about you before, so you have to find a way to demonstrate your special qualities and point out skills that are relevant to the job.

Only you can do that. Prospective employers expect that of you. Beyond the details, your resume must signal why someone should take a second look. It's up to you to cut through the clutter of the resumes of your competition. Keep in mind that employers may only spend thirty seconds looking at your resume, possibly only ten. If you haven't grabbed their attention, they will go on to another candidate.

Right up front, your passion and drive must come through. While you may have education and work credentials that are similar to other candidates, you really are different. And the resume, right from the get-go, must start to position you as someone special.

Make the recruiter pause and take the time to look more closely at you. With countless resumes showing up on the recruiter's screen, the sooner the better for you to stand out. To be realistic, after a quick glance or a slightly longer revue, most resumes will fall rather quickly into one of three buckets: "Not Interesting," "Maybe Later" and "Interesting." Clearly, you want to be in the latter. Anything else and you're a "no-show."

Is that a tough challenge? Absolutely. Which is why you should take the time to consider what makes you stand out.

Passion: Do you have a clear goal? Are you someone who has impressed professors, family and friends with brilliant thinking and analysis that proves your ability to focus on difficult ideas, drive through challenges and break new ground? Are you passionate when you believe in something?

Determination: Are you self-motivated? Someone who spends hours, days, weekends, summers and every other waking moment on your personal quest to accomplish great things and reach heights others only dream about?

Courage: Do you have a personal cause that matters to you? When you've met resistance, have you had the courage to stick with it? Analyzed the facts and argued intelligently? And then won?

Challenge: Are you someone who challenges the status quo and wants to do things differently? Do you see yourself revolutionizing the world, changing politics, influencing policy and creating change that improves lives?

Creativity: Do you believe that creative communication—whether through the arts, literature, music or writing—is at the core of mankind's ability to experience, learn and grow? Do you believe that ideas are at the heart of civilization?

What quality describes you? One of these? Or would it be something entirely different?

Is it genuine? If you asked those who know you well to give you a candid appraisal, would they agree?

And, of course, does it make you stand out?

... your resume must signal why someone should take a second look.

Career launches are rarely a seamless chain of events, but there is often a common thread that is visible early on. For me, passion, commitment and developing relationships—coupled with some luck—have been the differentiating factors.

Actually, my late teens were the start. I was focused and energized by competing in the junior tennis circuit. In addition to the rigors of training, I studied all facets of the game—from the science of racquet strings to sports psychology techniques.

Tennis led me to attend and play for the University of Pennsylvania, where it became abundantly clear that I was losing my passion for tennis and had only a very small possibility of professional tennis success. During my freshman and sophomore years, my time was consumed by coursework, and a career seemed like a distant worry. Being in an undergraduate business program, I conceptually desired a career in a dynamic corporate environment, but I had no bona fide plan.

While I had proven to be knowledgeable when passionate about a subject, this had not fully transferred into my coursework or career goals. During the summer following sophomore year, while at a train station, I recognized another former junior tennis player a few years my senior and began a conversation with him that lead to a critical mentorship. While luck placed us together, a willingness to face rejection allowed me to introduce myself. Critically, when taking a risk like this, it is important to remember that the worst scenario is that the person is simply not interested in speaking with you.

He was working in finance and described the contours of the industry. Given my background, he believed the finance industry would be the best learning ground for me to begin a career and one that would offer me options as I developed my skills. When I became excited about the prospect, he made it abundantly clear that spots at top firms are extremely selective. If I did not commit myself, I'd likely lose the opportunity. That evening, I began researching the finance industry and became obsessed. My passion increased as I learned more about the subject matter and the meaningful roles that might be available to me. After some hard work and luck, this ultimately led to me joining Goldman Sachs after graduation. I had an exceptional six-year experience at Goldman Sachs, prior to leaving the firm for an opportunity at a private investment firm where I remain today.

My career launch was a haphazard, multipronged combination of the below factors, which align with four of the key elements of this book.

Subject Matter Knowledge: Learn as much as you can about the industry, company and related current events. The internet offers immense free resources to help increase your subject matter fluency.

Network Outreach: Connect with everyone you possibly can and ask for help. At some point, everyone was in your position, and I have found that most people are willing to help. You only need one job, so don't fret about the occasional rejection.

Document Preparation: Perfect your resume and cover letter. Even the smallest typo or inconsistency can be taken as a negative signal about your attention to detail.

Interview Preparation: Refine your personal narrative and elevator pitch. Most interviews start with a question about your background and why you are interested in the role. Be ready. Finally, show your passion for something. Many interviews will delve into a topic on your resume. In my case, this circled back to tennis, where my ability to discuss the minutiae of racquet strings was viewed as a transferable ability to deeply understand and describe complex financial topics.

When I look back, if there is one element that matters most, it is passion. Passion drives you forward each step of the way, no matter the obstacles or challenges.

Keep pushing. Don't give up.

―――――――――― *II* ――――――――――
If I did not commit myself, I'd likely lose the opportunity.

9
AN OUTSIDE PERSPECTIVE

Be courageous and ask others
about your skills, abilities and strengths

Consider this: smart people—that's you—ask those they trust for their opinions.

Speak with those who know you well and ask them to tell you what they think about your work ethic, experiences, skills and, very importantly, the way you come across to others. There's nothing quite as insightful as an objective perspective from someone who knows you and cares enough to be candid, unemotional and straightforward.

Don't shy away because you fear being embarrassed. Yes, you might not like what you hear. It might make you feel uncomfortable. In the end, though, their objective insights will make you a stronger job candidate and put you in a better position to prepare a credible resume.

Be confident. Remember, you've likely done this at least once before. Think back to when you had to write a college essay that asked you to think through how you responded to an event in your life that made an impact. You probably asked for help then.

Over the years since then, you've matured. Life experiences have taken root and your interests have shifted. Those around you have seen the changes and recognize a greater maturity. They might be able to help you better understand and appreciate those experiences and instances that have helped shape how you think and your capabilities.

So go for it. Get that outside perspective. It will unquestionably make a big difference in your thinking. It will help you sharpen and focus your strengths. That will, in turn, lead to a better understanding of your career objectives and a clearer picture of the path to get there.

Talk to others. How do they view you when it comes to this baker's dozen of critical skills?

- Special talents, skills and training
- Education track record
- Interpersonal relationship building
- Self-confidence
- Presence
- Courage
- Initiative
- Teamwork
- Priority setting
- Work discipline
- Accomplishments

- Calm under pressure

- Analytical thinking

- Clear expression of thoughts and ideas

Remember, those who are willing to be candid with you are those who want you to succeed.

---------------------------***II***---------------------------

So go for it. Get that outside perspective.

10

THE ELEVATOR SPEECH

You have less than three minutes to sell yourself

Now it's time to test yourself. Are you clear about your goals, skills, talents and special qualities? Do they fit the kind of job you think you want?

You should be starting to have a clearer idea of how to position yourself. You've been through a self-assessment and asked for the opinions of those you trust.

Can you answer these questions?

- What's my passion? Does that translate into a job?

- What am I good at? What are my strengths?

- How about weaknesses? Will they be *job breakers* in some professions?

- What makes me stand out?

- If perception is reality, what do others think of me and my strengths?

- What elements are important to me in a job or career?

- What am I trained to do?

- What kinds of jobs do I really want?

Take the challenge: try describing yourself in three minutes, or what is commonly known as an elevator speech or an elevator pitch.

Imagine you just walked into an elevator in the offices of the one company where you most wanted to work. This is your ideal employer and perfect job. Standing right there in front of you is the CEO or the head of human resources, either one of whom is the one executive who could make sure your application was looked at seriously and could make the decision to hire you.

Holy smokes! You have less than three minutes until the elevator stops and your best chance at landing your dream job walks out the door. If you blow it, you alone are to blame.

So, what would you say when the CEO says, "Tell me about yourself."

That's the most common first interview question. Using a sports analogy, it's known as a softball. Your response needs to be a home run. Anything less than a strong and confident reply is worse than just being called out. It's actually game over.

Would you stumble? Have you thought about your career direction? How will you come across? What makes you special? What do you want to accomplish?

Simple questions? Not so if you haven't already worked through them. And your answer has to flow, without hesitation. Clarity and confidence are key. Just like any serious athlete who exercises and trains hard, you need to practice what you'd say in this scenario. It happens more often than you might think. Your practice and mental rehearsal will make the difference.

Without a good elevator pitch, you won't get far.

———————————— **//** ————————————

Holy smokes! You have less than three minutes until the elevator stops and your best chance at landing your dream job walks out the door. If you blow it, you alone are to blame.

11

SHORT IS TOUGH, BUT WORTH IT

Write your career goals or strengths in two or three sentences

When you sit down at the keyboard to start writing your resume, nothing will be more challenging and frustrating than penning those two to three sentences that describe your career goals or strengths.

However, take comfort. When you've done that, you've jumped the first writing hurdle and are on your way.

This step is tough for two reasons:

1. You have to have a clear picture of your strengths, passion and career direction. It's not easy to clarify those.

2. During all those years in college, most of your professors pushed expository writing as the single best format to use in writing essays. Expository writing lays out a problem or concept, discusses the details, facts and arguments, and then draws

a conclusion based on analysis. While expository writing works well for scholarly writing to ensure uniformity of format, objective analysis and step-by-step reasoning, this style won't help you hone in on your career goals in a few sentences. Moreover, you need the freedom to use language in a way that adds passion, since one of your key goals is to excite the reader to read more.

If you thought that writing a long essay was tough, think again. A short statement of goals and objectives is even tougher.

Take a lesson in brevity from one of our most celebrated writers, Henry David Thoreau. In 1857, he wrote, "Not that the story need be long, but it will take a long while to make it short."

Long before that, in 1656, French mathematician and philosopher Blaise Pascal apologized in the second to final paragraph of his famous 9,000-word "Provincial Letter XVI": "The present letter is a very long one, simply because I had no leisure to make it shorter."

The bottom line: your career goal must be a concise statement no longer than two or three sentences that looks to the future.

It should answer the question: Where to from here?

———————————————————**//**———————————————————

Not that the story need be long, but it will take a long while to make it short.

64

12

WRITE THE BEST COMMERCIAL EVER

No sesquipedalian permitted

Your resume is all about persuasion. It's little different from an award-winning, motivating ad. In this case, though, you're the product and your resume is your personal commercial, clear and direct about what you want to accomplish and, importantly, what you will bring to a company or organization.

Your goal is to make the reader determined and eager to meet you in person, because you grabbed their attention and built excitement about your potential.

But you only get one chance to impress. The challenge you face is that everybody gets bored quickly. You have to capture the reader's interest in the first few words or else you're not getting a second glance. As it is, most people reading a resume won't spend more than thirty seconds on it. With nothing exciting or intriguing, it's ready for delete and the trash bin.

Here are some guidelines:

- Write from the heart, talking about something that moves you to excel.
- Be expressive, not hesitant to evoke emotion.
- Make it sound like you.
- Don't be pretentious.
- Express clear thoughts.
- Make a statement that is bigger than you or the job you want.

Be especially careful in selecting the words you use:

- Think every word through carefully—a well-written resume speaks volumes about clear thinking.
- Write in the active voice. Absolutely no passive verbs permitted.
- Select words that mean something, not those that just fill space.
- Use simple words. A well-chosen, short word is often stronger and more impressive.
- Stay away from jargon. Professionals see through buzzwords that some might be tempted to use to make themselves seem smarter.
- Don't write like your philosophy professor or the author of a scientific journal.
- And don't make spelling or grammar mistakes —they are an instant turnoff.

Above all, no sesquipedalian ever. "What's a sesquipe-dalian?" you ask. Well, you've seen plenty of them before: words that are designed to sound important but are essentially hollow. They might seem great at a glance—long and elegant—but without much substance.

Once you're finished with your first draft, put it aside for a day. Come back to it. Be your toughest critic. Revise and edit. Check spelling and grammar. Put it aside again. Revise again. When you like it, give it to someone else to read.

Words are powerful. Use them well. It's important to get them right. After all, they're the key to a persuasive resume.

———————————————— *//* ————————————————
"What's a sesquipedalian?" you ask.

13
CAREER GOALS

Your passion and drive
made practical

No one can write your career goals or strengths quite like you. The passion and drive that will set you apart from other candidates are intensely personal. You have the best perspective from which to share the experiences—education, work, personal interests and life—that have shaped you and now point you toward the job you want and the kind of work you will find rewarding.

Here are some career goal examples that will give you a sense of how to incorporate your passion and drive.

- **"Digital technology has shaped our lives like never before. Working for a dynamic digital company is my goal.** With an undergraduate degree in computer science, I have a deep appreciation for the vital role that technology plays in our lives today, especially from the perspective of access to information and building knowledge."

- **"I am always looking for answers.** I know the importance of research to developing a deeper understanding of how ideas shape our lives. My studies have helped me appreciate the role that opinion research plays in decision-making at all levels. My career goal is to work with a leading research firm or institute."

- **"As one of six children, I have always known that my career would be in teaching.** I believe in the importance of helping children develop confidence in their own abilities and encouraging them to stretch themselves. Preschool education is my passion because it is there that enthusiasm for learning first starts."

- **"My goal is to work with a global financial services firm.** My studies in financial management and internships at capital management and investment firms have inspired me to develop a career where I can put my skills to work in international finance—where global politics, finance and business meet."

- **"As a dean's list student with a concentration in marketing and a Division I college athlete, I know that self-discipline and hard work are critical to success.** My goal is to join a manufacturing business where my work ethic and dedication can help the company grow by opening new markets and building sales."

- **"Ever since I was a child, I have been drawn to the oceans and the role they play in our lives.** My career goal is to work in an organization whose purpose is to ensure the safe and plentiful supply of seafood. I know this would be an exciting job. It is fast growing in importance, especially given rapidly expanding fish production, concerns about safety and the depletion of species and the pivotal role of fish in diet and health."

- "With a bachelor's degree in economics, I understand the importance of the private sector in creating opportunities for people to have successful lives, support their families and build wealth. My goal is to work in a bank and put my skills to work assisting customers to improve their lives."

- "Building on my degree in political science and my fluency in Spanish, I am eager to put my skills to use working as a paralegal in a Washington, DC, law firm. As federal policy and rule changes have a growing impact on our daily lives, there is no area more dynamic and important to each of us."

- "My passion is to insure thoughtful conversation between people of all ages and members of the scientific community. Clear and simple communications are crucial to developing the kind of understanding and sharing of information that has become so vital to appreciating the impact of science in our daily lives. I see myself in a career where science education plays a pivotal role."

- **"The education of students with learning disabilities has a special place in my heart.** I have held summer jobs as a tutor and academic coach, where I discovered my passion for helping young people gain self-confidence and reach their full potential. I've learned that I can help others by providing resources, a positive influence and the social skills needed to grow. Working as a full-time special education teacher is my goal."

The purpose behind illustrating the above examples is to illustrate how you can use your passion—and the source or reason behind it—and demonstrate how it has driven you to focus on a unique career direction.

Undoubtedly, yours will be different. But in the best of situations, the intensity of your drive to accomplish great things will help you express your career goals.

The passion and drive that will set you apart from other candidates are intensely personal.

14

SKILLS AND AREAS OF EXCELLENCE

"Hunger," "life" and *"work" skills* put to work

Landing a job is in great measure an economic agreement. The proposition you offer is that you are someone who brings potential, enthusiasm, training or a definable skill that will add value to a company or organization. In turn, that company or organization agrees to pay you a salary to have the benefit of your talents to help it reach its goals.

This is true whether you are speaking with a public entity or a private company, whether they have an active recruiting effort underway or there are no immediate openings. It doesn't matter whether your interview comes because of a reference from a friend or colleague or a posting on an online job board.

Are you someone whom a company or organization wants to hire because it believes you can deliver and help it be even more successful?

When most employers look at entry-level candidates, they look for signals that provide insights into whether you have three different kinds of skills:

1. **Hunger skills:** Are you enthusiastic? Excited about the job opportunity? Committed? Hungry to prove to yourself and others that you will get up early, work long hours, keep at it until the job gets done and follow up even when it gets tough?

2. **Life skills:** They need to know that you will get to work on time—or better yet, early—be responsible, dedicated and trustworthy; bring the right values to the workplace; and function as a member of the team.

3. **Work skills:** They want to see some proof that you have started to develop specific skills and may already have some experience that will be valuable. Of course, employers recognize that entry-level employees require training, either formal or on the job.

Without all three, there's no job for you.

If you want to stand out, showcase your skills every chance you get. Using a well-organized and structured format for your resume creates the opportunity to do just that in a number of places. When you discuss your work experience, look for ways to point out your accomplishments and how your skills helped you excel.

And when you recap special interests, awards, honors or community activities, focus on those that tell the reader about a skill you learned or put to work that made you especially valuable.

The bottom line is: if you want the reader of your resume to walk away with a positive view about you and what you can do for their organization, you have to be sure what you bring to the table is clear. Don't hope that they will discover your skills on their own. If you don't tell them, they won't know. And if you think they will go out of their way to find out how you can help them, forget it. Even the most skilled and focused interviewer doesn't take the time to do what you should have done for yourself.

... you are someone who brings potential, enthusiasm, training or a definable skill that will add value to a company or organization.

15

THE ORGANIZING PRINCIPLE BEHIND A STRONG RESUME FORMAT

Hit hard upfront with a powerful and quick read

Think about the last short story or novel you read. Did that opening paragraph or first few pages grab your attention? Or think about the last television show or latest movie you saw. How long did it take for you to decide that it was or wasn't for you? Or think back on your reaction to the first few beats of the latest song to drop.

Very likely, your reaction was pretty quick. That's why the subheads for bestselling books are written as teasers. And why ads use dramatic footage or action to get you to buy whatever they're selling. Or why good commercials hit you hard in less than fifteen seconds so that the images are memorable and you are inclined to look for their product. Or they use heart-pumping music and graphic images to get your attention right from the beginning.

Take those experiences and imagine a human resources professional, recruiter or manager who is looking to hire a new staff member and is now faced with reading through hundreds of resumes.

Yours has to cut through the clutter, or else it will be lost in the sheer volume of resumes that human resources or a recruiter receives online.

Unfortunately, unless an employer has asked you to send a video or some kind of work sample, you do not have the benefit of drama, rock 'n' roll or the roar of racing cars.

Your resume has to do the trick and get you in the door for an interview.

It has to be well thought-through and structured so that it communicates a powerful and special message about you ... right from the top.

With that in mind, strong resumes follow a few important *organizing principles*.

- It's what's upfront that matters most.

- Your goal is to immediately attract the attention of anyone who picks up your resume, offering a thoughtful perspective and communicating what makes you special.

- Use smart language. Push crisp, active verbs and a confident approach to the forefront.

- Be sure to link your thinking and career goals to what is important to your prospective employer.

- Keep the format simple. Make it easy for the eye to follow details, even with a quick glance.

- Select a structure that is flexible enough to be adapted to a number of potential job applications, especially when key words and concepts need to be emphasized.

Never forget: what you are selling is you. Your resume is a sales and marketing document. Don't fall into the trap of thinking that your resume is simply a chronology of every job you ever had.

Make it relevant and concise. Each entry must have a purpose and everything must come together as part of a concise story that gets you in the door for that crucial first interview.

Without that first interview, there won't be a second. And then, certainly, there's no job offer coming your way.

------------------------------ **"** ------------------------------

Never forget: what you are selling is you.

16

A STRONG, FLEXIBLE AND SIMPLE RESUME FORMAT

The focus is on content: strengths, skills and accomplishments

When you decide on a format, never forget that your resume is a sales tool and marketing document. The format should be flexible enough for you to emphasize what you want. After all, *you* are what's being sold.

Your focus must be on content: your strengths and skills, with a strong emphasis on your accomplishments. This is not the place for a recap of every job you had. Frankly, no one is interested.

Recruiters are interested in what you've accomplished and what you can accomplish going forward.

Moreover, a strong resume discusses those activities and jobs that directly relate to the job you are looking for. If you include too much, you run the risk of appearing as if you are either adding items just to fill space or are not disciplined in looking at which experiences have direct relevance to the job you are after.

Use a clean and simple format to make an impact, keeping it to the point and credible.

Don't be tempted to make it fancy, with colored ink or paper or use anything other than a clean design.

If you are determined to include a photo, don't use it as the centerpiece of your resume.

At the outset, don't use what is often described as a *template*. Resume templates are way more restricting than a simple format because templates are pre-designed forms that have specific places for including certain material that you may or may not want or be able to include. Templates can tempt you to add irrelevant material.

Play to your strengths. You are a unique individual, and what works for others might not work for you.

So when you decide on a format, focus on content and flexibility.

Take a look at some sample formats in the Appendix.

They are variations of the same concept: putting your goals and skills up front, followed by your education and then by the jobs you have had and accomplishments you have made.

The sample resumes provide flexible formats that allow you to include or not include certain skills and areas of excellence, depending on your qualifications and the *key words* identified in the job posting. Explore different resume styles with a view toward drawing the recruiter's eye toward your best qualities.

They also show you how to emphasize one element of your education or your work experience over another. For example, one format places your degree before the college or university name, depending on which aspect of your education you believe is more important or impressive. Or vice versa. And in another example, one format emphasizes where you worked over the dates of your employment. When deciding which format to use, keep in mind that continuity of work over many summers sends an important signal about your *work skills*.

Regardless, these formats can be easily updated and adapted as you apply to different jobs. And the core content can remain the same.

If these formats don't work for you, ask others for suggestions or build one of your own in Microsoft Word.

Regardless of the format you decide to use, though, remember that it's the content that counts.

Use a clean and simple format to make an impact, keeping it to the point and credible.

17

ONE SIZE DOESN'T FIT ALL

Tailor your resume to each job

There's hardly a job posting that doesn't urge applicants to ensure that their resume responds to the job specs.

And you can understand why. With a simple posting on the internet—either directly from an employer or from a search site—it is not uncommon for a hundred applicants to respond within the first few days or so. And the number continues to climb every day thereafter for about two weeks.

With that kind of competition, if your application doesn't deserve a second look, you're out of luck.

Reviewing resumes by hand is mostly history. Artificial intelligence, algorithms and machine learning are here to stay. Digital programs look for key words, most of which are specifically noted in the posting itself. This moves the process for evaluating candidates along much more quickly and leaves little sympathy for those resumes missing key qualifications.

So when you find a job that interests you, check twice. First, check to see if you have some of the qualifications. Second, check to ensure that those qualifications are front and center on your resume.

More often, this means that portions of your resume—while they may be very thoughtful and well presented—will not suffice and need to be tailored each time you send it out.

If not tailored, it's sort of like launching your resume into a dark hole once you've pressed "send." The proof is in the disappointment of many when they send out a hundred or more resumes and don't get even one reply.

So, what sections of your resume need to be flexible enough that you can tailor goals and qualifications to match a particular job or another? Certainly not the factual sections, because they must be an accurate account of school and work history and cannot be modified.

However, there are other more subjective areas in your resume. Those are the ones about your goals, strengths, skills and areas of excellence that reflect your self-evaluation and aspirations. Keep in mind that you are just starting out on the job front. And as you hear about and explore a wider range of jobs, you will discover that you have skills or goals that you hadn't identified before. This is the same kind of career reflection and healthy reevaluation of your strengths that you will do at every stage of your career.

When you think about applying for a particular job and you review the qualifications demanded, take a close look at what you have said in those sections. Those areas, along with your cover letter, give you a chance to show-case how you view yourself and your qualifications for different jobs.

Remember, use your resume wisely. After all, it is the single most important tool for you to use to sell yourself and convince others of your potential.

Don't sell yourself short. There are more opportunities than you can imagine at the outset.

————————————————— **II** —————————————————

Artificial intelligence, algorithms and machine learning are here to stay.

PERSPECTIVE

RESUMES AND INTERVIEWS
What a recruiter needs to hear

JULIE BIBER

Managing director, executive recruitment
and search, Edelman

In my twenty-one years spent recruiting for Edelman, a leading global communications firm, I have always searched for talent who have what we call the *Edel-DNA*. These are certain critical qualities and long-held values that we see as core to our culture, history and continued success.

We want to hear how each candidate has demonstrated the pursuit of excellence, the courage to do the right thing, the freedom to remain always curious and the commitment to improve society.

Of course, we look for skills and experience, but we are also looking to see the depth of their core values and their work ethic.

Every day, our business demands ideas, creativity and finding solutions that others may have missed.

So, when I review resumes or prepare to interview candidates, I ask myself: Are they nimble? Are they scrappy? Are they humble? Are they ingenious?

As our founder, Dan Edelman, always said, "Each one of us is always an account executive … One of those who knows how to do, drive, and inspire work in themselves and others." He would then add: "Do the best work that stands out from all the others."

This kind of passion is critical.

A level of grit and perseverance, a collaborative spirit and a passion for the changing field of communications are all critical elements. When grounded in professionalism and integrity, this is a recipe for success.

I put a premium on one's ability to learn alongside their desire to grow. I am very bullish on people who are students of the business. A progressive mind-set is very compelling. An ability to swiftly problem-solve in complex situations is imperative. Thriving in a fast-paced culture with ambiguity is a must in talent we hire. It's important that candidates are able to provide examples of how they have handled similar kinds of situations.

My counsel is to always bring your value proposition to the table and share with me how it will set you apart. I want someone to tell me their personal story of accomplishments, challenges and goals. Diversification of experience, skills and background are of utmost importance. While a strong academic track is necessary, I want to know what the person has done in leadership roles and with purpose-driven work.

When I first look at resumes, I often ask myself:

- In what areas do these candidates excel? What are their accomplishments? What separates them from the others? Does anything jump out at me? What do their goals or strengths say about the values they will bring to us?

When I interview a candidate, I ask:

- What have you done that has illustrated leadership? When have you taken on more than what was asked of you? How have you tackled change or adversity? What companies do you admire and why?

No matter how tenured, it is important that a candidate has researched our firm prior to a conversation or meeting, in particular, spending time on our website, reading our CEO Richard Edelman's 6 A.M. blog and admiring our great work.

Don't forget: even if the timing of our job opportunity and your application may not fit right now, it certainly could in the future.

P.S. A sense of humor, warmth and bringing out the *real* you are highly recommended.

***

My counsel is to always bring your value proposition to the table and share with me how it will set you apart.

18

THE ESSENTIAL COVER LETTER

You and your passion

A word of caution: in case you might be tempted to skip the chance to write a strong cover letter to go with your resume and application, that would be a huge mistake.

In a world in which technology is taking over the job search process for many entry-level positions, some internet job postings give applicants the opportunity to opt in or out of providing a cover letter. This means that those who are not as eager or are just focused on sending out as many resumes as possible and hoping some will stick lose the opportunity to highlight their best qualities and communicate clearly to the reader why they are the right person for the job.

Think about it. Even the smartest and best-targeted resume can't possibly share all of your thinking or give you the chance to expand on the passion and understanding you have about the potential job. Resumes are not designed to be the place for you to share your thoughts about the more subjective aspects of your interest in a job or company.

By its design, your resume focuses on facts. The format limits what you can include because of available space and the amount of information you have to share. At this early stage of your career, you need to use the available space to highlight key words and present those facts that give your application essential work credentials: goals, skills, education, employment history and accomplishments.

Of necessity, the cover letter then becomes a critical component of your application.

First, it is just that—a *cover* letter. As such, it is more often than not the first thing a potential employer reads. It can very well set the scene for what the recruiter will read later in your resume and any other parts of your application.

Second, a strong cover letter gives you the chance to communicate your candidacy much more effectively. It makes for a strong first impression. It works best when you:

- Give a sense of why your passion about a particular job drives you.

- Share insights into why you care so strongly about the job and believe in its importance.

- Demonstrate your research and grasp of the company or organization where you are applying.

- Provide insights through your depth of thinking and clarity of expression.

- Showcase your written communication skills by using language succinctly and effectively.

- Reinforce your accomplishments and what you can do for a new employer.

The goal of a cover letter is to show the recruiter that you understand the organization, have thought about how you can fulfill the responsibilities of the job and are eager for the opportunity to add value to the organization through your hard work.

Bottom line: no job seeker can expect others to do the job for them, hoping that the recruiter will pick up all the right messages from your resume alone.

Success means landing the job, and no one can showcase yourself better than you can.

Don't skip the cover letter—even when a prospective employer says you can.

---***---

… the cover letter then becomes a critical component of your application.

19

ONLINE JOB SEARCH

"Key words" make the internet
work for you

Mass marketing of job opportunities has become the norm.
The internet has dramatically changed the way jobs are posted and applicants apply. Clicks have replaced emails, letters, phone calls and introductory meetings. Whether working at a search firm or on the staff of a company, recruiters are able to gather as many as one hundred resumes in just a few days.

The sheer number of applicants makes it almost impossible for a recruiter to review each application individually, let alone respond. While applicants may receive an automated, one-line email acknowledging that their application has been received, many times that's all the feedback anyone hears, and it feels like your resume has simply disappeared.

Technology has made it possible for recruiters to not only streamline the process but build in a level of objectivity that didn't exist before. It makes the early stages of the application and recruitment process less of a human function and more like a machine, creating efficiencies for the recruiter and demanding more specificity from the applicant.

To move the process along quickly, recruiters have become adept at identifying *key words*: words that give them an early indication of a prospective employee's skill and experience set.

Look at LinkedIn, for example. It makes a bold statement about its job search platform: "Over 20 million jobs. Let's find the right one for you." It goes on to say that you can "search jobs—see jobs that fit your background, experience and interests [and] tell 2.8 million talent professionals what you're interested in."

As a job search tool, LinkedIn is one of the most powerful because it's interactive. You can leverage it to learn about opportunities and get your resume and cover letter in front of the right employers.

However, getting started and making it work for you means you need to focus on words and skills that an employer has identified as being critical to success in the posted job. Without them, you're not likely to get very far. Recruiters who use artificial intelligence to narrow the list of candidates identify *key words* that indicate a candidate has a particular skill or ability, and discerning what those words are is the first hurdle.

The obvious first step is to look at potential job listings in your field of interest and make a list of requirements that employers identify, paying careful attention to what words and phrases they use. With that in hand, ask yourself: Do I have any of those qualities or any experience in those areas? If so, use their language in your cover letter and resume to make your application stand out and pass the AI threshold.

You will likely have to prepare more than one resume, each one tailored to the qualifications of a particular job.

The internet is a powerful tool in a job search that works best when you are specific.

———————————————— *II* ————————————————

Clicks have replaced emails, letters, phone calls and introductory meetings.

20

NETWORKING

Put relationships to work

As you focus your energies on preparing the best resume possible, take a break, step back and put yourself in the shoes of an employer.

Imagine the challenge when—after clicking through countless resumes, interview reports and reference checks—it's now decision time.

All other things being equal, what would tip the scale toward the job offer heading in your direction?

The answer's a quick one: relationships.

Many employers encourage their employees to recommend candidates when there is an opening. Moreover, more and more employers offer a bonus if that recommendation turns into a new hire.

Common wisdom will tell you that, if you have a productive employee who is valued, he or she would be more likely to know others who have the same qualities and values. And by getting a reference from someone you know, the company or organization can save some of the cost of a search.

Every recruiter will tell you the same thing: build relationships by networking. Talk to your friends, talk to the parents of your friends and talk to those who might be in a position to know of job openings and have their own sphere of contacts, some of whom might also know of openings and could recommend you.

Spread the network far and wide. And don't be shy. You never know who will know someone who knows someone who has a job opening or would serve as a reference for you.

It's no surprise then that the underlying concept behind any online job site is networking. The same holds for more traditional recruiters who ask around when searching for candidates and take comfort in a recommendation.

Again, look at LinkedIn as an example. When you use LinkedIn to search for jobs or when it notifies you of a potential job because you've already outlined your career goals and skills, it also shares with you your LinkedIn connections who currently work for that organization. The goal is to give you access to those who might be able put in a good word for you.

You have to have the skills and go through a complete application and interview process, but with a thumbs-up from someone who is already working there, you've put yourself in a better position to land that job.

So build a network. Ask around. Be confident and eager. Be courageous. These are essential techniques to build relationships and get a leg up in your job search.

———————————————**//**———————————————

So build a network. Ask around. Be confident and eager. Be courageous.

21

"COMPLETED STAFF WORK"

Make it easy for others to help you

If you've never heard of *completed staff work*, now is the perfect time to learn about this leadership technique. It can play an important role in your job search and throughout your career.

The term *completed staff work* is reported to have had its origin in the military during wartime. Research points to memoranda issued by the US Army in 1942 and by the Royal Canadian Army in 1943. Since that time, the concept has been adopted by governments and corporations. The reason is clear: it has proven to be a very effective process for moving from discussion to solution to action. The military procedure is that a staff officer is delegated the responsibility of analyzing each of the elements involved in a decision and making a recommendation. The mandate is that this analysis needs to be so thorough and thoughtful that the officer in authority can simply read, approve and set the decision in motion.

At first glance, some might say that this has little to do with your job search. But not so. In fact, it can be a critical factor and make the difference between success and failure.

Think about it. If you have a relationship with someone who might be helpful in your search, it might be a good idea to ask that person to weigh in on your behalf as a reference. In short, you are looking for an endorsement of your skills and abilities from someone who is credible as an added push to get your resume to the top of the pile.

But how do you get them to do that for you, especially if timing is important and everyone you ask is likely to be very busy? In addition, how can you best equip them to put forward your candidacy in a convincing way?

The best technique is to think of it from the perspective of *completed staff work*. So get ready to send them a thoughtful email or letter, outlining the position you are going for and your qualifications. Make it thorough and well written. If you write that letter well, the goal is that they can simply put their own email or note on top of yours and forward or send it to their contact as a strong endorsement of your candidacy. This means they can help you without needing to do very much.

In the letter, talk about your interest in the company or organization that posted the job and what you know about the opportunity. Share thoughts about your career goals and how this job fits in, and don't hesitate to talk about your passion for this kind of work and how you believe it impacts you and others. Go into detail about your qualifications for the job and the skills required. Recognize the importance of delivering value. Above all, communicate a sense of excitement about the job and organization. And do it all in one page.

In effect, by helping them, you are making it easy for them to help you.

After all, it's not realistic to expect someone else to write a full endorsement letter for you. They might not have the time and or know enough about you or the opportunity to be credible. You need to do it for yourself. If you don't, you won't get that endorsement.

Completed staff work helps others help you.

//

… by helping them, you are making it easy for them to help you.

22

BEFORE YOU CLICK "APPLY"

Leave nothing to chance

You've now thought it all through, you're pleased with your resume and cover letter and you're just about ready to click "apply" and post your application.

Wait a moment. Step away and read what you've written one last time. Try your best to picture what those words say about you.

Did you answer the critical question: Why you?

Did you share enough of your thinking and accomplishments that someone can envision what you could do for them?

So, did you . . .

tell your story . . .

- from the heart
- about your passion
- about what you've accomplished so far and what you believe you can accomplish

keep it . . .

- focused
- authentic
- straightforward
- honest

communicate effectively . . .

- with conviction
- with active verbs
- with short sentences
- with no pretentious or hollow words
- clearly and to the point

check for . . .

- grammar and spelling—no typos
- accuracy

Now pause one last time. Is there anything else?

Are there any other points you would emphasize if you had the chance? Anything about your family, summer work or college experiences that tell a unique story? Work ethic, skills, teamwork, leadership, drive or lessons learned about getting along with others? Jot them down. They might be very important when you get that interview.

How about if you are asked for references and contacts at your summer jobs. Do you have those names—with correct spelling, addresses, phone numbers and email addresses—readily at hand? If all goes well, you will need them quickly.

Leave nothing to chance. Make sure it is your very best. And then click "apply."

———————————————— **//** ————————————————

Did you answer the critical question: Why you?

23

INTERVIEW PREP

Do your research and rehearse
… then rehearse again

You've reached a critical point in your job search. Your resume was well received. The date for your interview is set. It will likely last about forty-five minutes.

While it's unlikely that you would be hired without an in-person interview, don't be surprised if that initial meeting is a *virtual* one.

Technology has invaded the interview process, saving both candidate and company time and resources. But not having to travel and sit down with a recruiter or employer is no reason to take the discussion any less seriously. Or prepare any less vigorously.

Every interaction with a prospective employer is equally crucial.

Your goal is to project confidence, knowledge, an understanding of both the organization and the job itself and, importantly, a palpable level of energy along with insights into your character.

A strong interview is your goal. Anything less will leave you on the sidelines.

So, how do you prep for that interview?

Research and rehearse is the answer.

First, research the organization: understand its business, goals, customers, values, culture and reputation. Carefully think through why this particular job is for you and what you can bring.

Remember, the interview is your chance to make a strong impression. So organize your thinking and take notes so you don't leave anything out.

Second, rehearse. Imagine you are sitting with the recruiter, the head of human resources or even a chief executive. What kinds of questions could you be asked about your successes, failures, goals, passion, work experience and career focus? Perhaps you'll be asked to comment on a few workplace scenarios, such as your thoughts on how to get along with colleagues when there is conflict or how you would ensure the work was completed, even when the customary end of the workday had since passed. Surely, you'll also be asked what you know about the organization itself.

Think through the range of possible questions you might be asked, jot them down, and take them seriously. Then rehearse your responses.

Don't be put off by some of the stranger questions you might have read about online or heard about from others. They are rare. Most interviewers are straightforward and focused on giving every candidate a fair chance.

Your best rehearsal will include asking a friend to role-play as your interviewer, asking questions and listening to your answers. Encourage candor from whomever is helping you. Don't be embarrassed when your answer isn't good enough. Try again. It's the best way to improve.

Use your cell phone to video yourself as you rehearse. There's nothing more valuable than seeing yourself in action, especially when you are under pressure and responding to questions. It's a sure test of how prepared you really are.

Make your mistakes during rehearsal, not when it really counts. There are rarely any interview do-overs.

Keep in mind that the most constructive interview is a dialog where there is a thoughtful give-and-take. The interviewer asks and listens. And you take the opportunity to ask questions and listen.

Be ready to ask questions. Well in advance, prepare some questions that you want to ask about the organization, culture and any issues that surfaced in your research that you would like to explore. In fact, at some point before the interview is over, every interviewer will ask you the standard: "Do you have any questions for me?"

If preparation for the interview means research and rehearsal, divide that task into four parts:

1. Research the company that posted the job:

- Do your research well, starting with the organization's website.

- Spend time searching online to gain a deeper understanding of the organization's reputation, earnings and products or services.

- Review press reports, analyst coverage and the chairman's letter in the annual report.

- Use social media to learn how the company is perceived and follow it on LinkedIn.

- Memorize key aspects of the business, including competition, strategic direction and values.

- Be ready to answer questions about how you view the organization and whether you believe you would find working there exciting and challenging.

- Develop questions of your own.

2. Prepare yourself to make a strong first impression:

- Be sure to dress for the job you want.

- Remember to smile, shake hands firmly and look each person in the eye.

- Be confident and remember names.

- Start taking notes immediately. It visibly demonstrates that you are paying attention and care.

3. Concentrate on the value you will add and what you can accomplish:

- Hone in on just three of your skills or special qualities that you think are the most important for the job and be sure to emphasize them. Make them memorable.

- Rehearse how those skills and areas of excellence relate specifically to the job.
- Rehearse how your passion, studies and work experiences have helped shape your career choices.
- Rehearse how you can thoughtfully share insights about your other strengths and weaknesses, and how you will add value and assist the organization in reaching its goals.
- Be ready to explain any gaps in your resume.

4. Close with a lasting impression:

- Be ready to close strong, since interviewers often remember both the first and last image they have of a candidate.
- Emphasize how impressed you are with the organization and its reputation.
- Emphasize how eager you are to add value to the organization, and how, with your skills, education and experience, you believe you will be successful.

Preparation makes for champions. World-class athletes exercise, train and run drills. Concert artists rehearse. And race-car drivers hit the track for practice runs.

You should be doing nothing less.

——————————————————— **//** ———————————————————

The interviewer asks and listens. And you take the opportunity to ask questions and listen.

24

AFTER THE INTERVIEW

There's no job without your personal follow-up

The interview may be over but follow up can be the "make or break" for your candidacy.

Yes. There's much written about the job search and no lack of thoughts on how to ace the interview. You may have followed the best advice: connecting with the interviewer, demonstrating your knowledge of the organization, illustrating your accomplishments, showing your enthusiasm, voicing your passion and commitment to the job and reassuring the interviewer that you have the determination to accomplish whatever it takes to create success all around.

And of course, you will have closed each interview with your own form of thank you, perhaps something along these lines: "I'm excited about the opportunity, eager to speak further and look forward to hearing from you."

And all of that certainly is crucial.

However, there's yet another step, one that can reinforce a positive interview, perhaps even salvage one that didn't go quite so well, or, if neglected, sound the end to your candidacy. That step is your personal follow-up. Without it, you're not likely to get very far.

Follow-up needs to be more than a quick email with a perfunctory, one-line "Thanks for the chance to meet, and I look forward to speaking further."

You need to raise some substantive issues that came up in the interview and either ask a question or share an observation. That means you will have had to pay close attention to the issues raised in the interview and recall important elements of the discussion, which might be valuable to refer to later.

Think of it this way: the goal of follow-up is much more than the politeness of a thank you. It's twofold: First, to extend the discussion so that meeting you remains memorable. And second, to further demonstrate your understanding of the job and what you can accomplish.

It doesn't have to be long—only a few short paragraphs—but it does have to be thoughtful. You might want to look for ways to share additional observations about one of these in your follow-up note:

- The interview discussion itself.

- Questions you were asked that you can or should expand upon.

- Impressions of the organization and the way you perceive its values and focus on talent.

- Thoughts that came to you after the interview was completed.

- Special skills or experience you bring to the team.

- The source of your passion for that particular kind of work to make it clear that it's more than just a job to you.

- Above all, make it meaningful.

A few words along these lines in a follow-up note can put you at the top of the list.

―――――――――――――― **//** ――――――――――――――

Think of it this way: the goal of follow-up is much more than the politeness of a thank you.

PERSPECTIVE

INSIGHTS FROM A BOSS

PATRICK FORD

Professional in residence, University of Florida

Congratulations!

You made it through the labyrinth of HR recruiters, their checklists, search engine *key words* and AI algorithms.

Finally your resume gets to me—the boss.

You're hired, right?

Not quite.

This is the most challenging stage. Your resume likely came to me from HR along with some other candidates, all of whom checked the right boxes and might even have relationships at the company through family, friends, other connections or university alumni. And it probably arrived in the course of a hectic day when there's too little time to focus on too many priorities.

In short, your resume has seconds to stand out if you want to inspire me to read on or, better yet, put you on the short list for final interviews.

Just how does that happen?

After years of looking at hundreds of resumes, interviewing candidates and mentoring those who are looking for a job, here's one clue: *find a way to help me see why I should get to know you.*

This is an essential component when you really want that job. It helps move your candidacy from a piece of paper to a "must meet."

No doubt that's hard to do. It takes creativity and a large measure of introspection when putting together your resume.

One of my favorite resumes of all time came from a graduating senior at a leading university. She had impeccable accomplishments: a 4.0 GPA, three impressive internships over the past summers, two leadership roles in relevant campus organizations and more.

She had me interested from the start.

But here's what stuck out and moved her to top of the candidate list: In the lower section of her resume, she had a box with an unusual heading, "My Hidden Career." That's where she described the YouTube channel she had created on her own time. In a short time, she had 13,000 subscribers!

Beyond showcasing this kind of accomplishment, it told me she's the type of person who sees an opportunity and makes it happen, as opposed to staying on the sidelines and just wishing.

And it convinced me I needed to meet this student before someone else snatched her up.

Is all this a lot to expect from a single piece of paper? Absolutely. But if you want to get on that short list, it's your job to make sure that you make me want to meet you.

As you put together your resume and prepare for an interview, follow these guidelines:

- **Demonstrate the strengths and character of your personal brand.** Be clear why those attributes relate to the company's needs and culture. Bosses don't just look for core skills. We look for signs about character, work ethic and propensity to learn.

- **Resist the urge to recite every task you've performed at every job.** Instead, focus on your special accomplishments in relevant jobs and campus activities. You say you handled social media during your internship?

What results can you credibly cite? You wrote for a community newspaper during senior year? Mention one or two pieces you wrote and why they mattered.

- **Make it easy to read.** When I warn a student she may have as little as two seconds of the boss's attention, I say it from firsthand experience. When pressed for time, I tend to move right past a wordy, poorly organized resume. I assume, if it got through the basic screening, that the candidate is smart and probably met the general criteria for the role. But I just don't have the time to dwell on it. The onus is on you, the candidate, to enable me to see at a glance what makes you exceptional and why it matters to my business.

Adding to all those challenges, HR and bosses like me expect entry-level resumes to be one page.

So, last but not least by any means, keep these in mind about your resume:

1. Do your research to make sure you customize your resume to highlight the credentials that address the stated job description and the company's priorities.

2. Keep the layout simple so that the reader's eyes move quickly and naturally to your key value proposition. Think about effective magazine covers or movie trailers that make it hard to resist wanting more. They don't have the time or space to tell you about all the wonderful things

inside, but they sure do know how to grab you in seconds.

Yes, this is all a lot for one page.

But like others before you, you, too, can make it happen and land that job.

———————————— **‖** ————————————

… here's one clue: *find a way to help me see why I should get to know you.*

———————————————————————

25

WHAT'S NEXT?

Take charge and prepare
for the unexpected

Even your very best effort must have a backup.

Things may not go quite as smoothly as you hoped.

Rarely in the world of business and politics does anything stand still. Strategic and operational goals may need be revised. Performance or position in the marketplace may take a turn for better or worse. An employer's hiring plans may change.

Moreover, it's only realistic to anticipate that other qualified candidates may be in the mix, some of whom may have relationships that you do not. And there's always the element of chemistry.

Even if you believe the interview went very well, you should continue to move forward on other job opportunities and alternatives. You never know how things will turn out, and the final decision on whether to offer you the job is in the hands of your prospective employer, not you.

Just as you've taken charge of your resume and done everything to position yourself for the job search so far, don't stop now.

Be ready for the unexpected.

Remember the admonition of Nicholas Murray Butler, American statesman, Noble Peace Prize recipient and twelfth president of Columbia University, who said in a speech on March 21, 1931:

> The vast population of this earth, and indeed nations themselves, may readily be divided into three groups. There are the few who make things happen, the many more who watch things happen, and the overwhelming majority who have no notion of what happens. Every human being is born into this third and largest group; it is for himself, his environment and his education to determine whether he shall rise to the second group or even to the first.

So in a world where there are "those who make things happen, those who watch things happen and those who wonder what happened," make sure you are among those who make things happen.

After all, your job hangs in the balance.

---- **//** ----

You never know how things will turn out, and the final decision on whether to offer you the job is in the hands of your prospective employer, not you.

APPENDIX ONE

SAMPLE RESUME FORMATS

Check out these sample resume formats.

They're simple and give you the opportunity to highlight your career goals, strengths, skills, areas of excellence, *key words*, education, accomplishments and work experience.

If these don't work for you, ask others for suggestions or build one of your own in Microsoft Word.

Regardless of the format you decide to use, though, remember that it's the content that counts.

First, Middle Initial and Last Name

Email Address | Cell Phone | LinkedIn

College/University Address
Street, City, State Zip

Home Address
Street, City, State Zip

Career Goal | Career Strengths: This is a focused paragraph of no more than three powerful, personal sentences that capture:

- Your motivation to focus on a particular career or job—your passion
- Education, training, work experience, internships, or unique interests that led you in this direction
- Importance of the work/career

Skills | Areas of Excellence: Life/work/hunger skills | accomplishments/experience from work or internships | work strengths | team experience | specialized interests | leadership | language fluency | key words that address specific job skills noted in a particular posting

---

Education

Bachelor of Arts/Sciences—Specific Degree Title
College or University Name—City, State—Dates of attendance and expected graduation month/year

- GPA: 0.00 / 4.0
- Dean's list/academic honors/teaching or research assistantship/varsity sports teams/awards

Special Studies—Name and Location

- Dates
- Specialized study program description

Work Experience and Accomplishments (including summer work and internships)

From-to-Date **Name of Company or Organization—City, State**
Title and/or specific role

- Describe your responsibilities and what you accomplished in three bullets of one line each
- Use active voice, not passive
- Stay away from jargon and meaningless words

From-to-Date **Name of Company or Organization—City, State**
Title and/or specific role

- Describe your responsibilities and what you accomplished in three bullets of one line each
- Use active voice, not passive
- Stay away from jargon and meaningless words

From-to-Date **Name of Company or Organization—City, State**
Title and/or specific role

- Describe your responsibilities and what you accomplished in three bullets of one line each
- Use active voice, not passive
- Stay away from jargon and meaningless words

Leadership/Awards/Activities/Special Interests/Volunteer Community Service

- One sentence description of each
- One sentence description of each

129

First, Middle Initial and Last Name
Email Address | Cell Phone | LinkedIn

College/University Address
Street, City, State Zip

Home Address
Street, City, State Zip

Career Goal | Career Strengths: This is a focused paragraph of no more than three powerful, personal sentences that capture:
- Your motivation to focus on a particular career or job—your passion
- Education, training, work experience, internships, or unique interests that led you in this direction
- Importance of the work/career

Skills | Areas of Excellence:
- Life/work/hunger skills
- Specialized interests
- Leadership
- Accomplishments/experience from work or internships

- Language fluency
- Work strengths
- Teamwork experience
- Key words that address specific job skills noted in a particular posting

---

Education

College or University Name—City, State
Bachelor of Arts/Sciences—Specific Degree Title—Dates of attendance and expected graduation
- GPA: 0.00 / 4.0
- Dean's list/academic honors/teaching or research assistantship/varsity sports teams/awards

Special Studies—Name and Location
- Dates
- Specialized study program description

Work Experience and Accomplishments (including summer work and internships)

Name of Company or Organization—City, State   From-to-Date
Title and/or specific role
- Describe your responsibilities and what you accomplished in three bullets of one line each
- Use active voice, not passive
- Stay away from jargon and meaningless words

Name of Company or Organization—City, State   From-to-Date
Title and/or specific role
- Describe your responsibilities and what you accomplished in three bullets of one line each
- Use active voice, not passive
- Stay away from jargon and meaningless words

Name of Company or Organization—City, State   From-to-Date
Title and/or specific role
- Describe your responsibilities and what you accomplished in three bullets of one line each
- Use active voice, not passive
- Stay away from jargon and meaningless words

Leadership/Awards/Activities/Special Interests/Volunteer Community Service
- One sentence description of each
- One sentence description of each

First, Middle Initial and Last Name
Email Address | Cell Phone | LinkedIn

College/University Address
Street, City, State Zip

Home Address
Street, City, State Zip

Career Goal | Career Strengths: This is a focused paragraph of no more than three powerful, personal sentences that capture:

- Your motivation to focus on a particular career or job—your passion
- Education, training, work experience, internships, or unique interests that led you in this direction
- Importance of the work/career

Skills | Areas of Excellence:

- ✓ Life/work/hunger skills
- ✓ Specialized interests
- ✓ Leadership
- ✓ Accomplishments/experience from work or internships

- ✓ Language fluency
- ✓ Work strengths
- ✓ Teamwork experience
- ✓ Key words that address specific job skills noted in a particular posting

Education

Bachelor of Arts/Sciences—Specific Degree Title
College or University Name—City, State—Dates of attendance and expected graduation month/year

- GPA: 0.00 / 4.0
- Dean's list/academic honors/teaching or research assistantship/varsity sports teams/awards

Special Studies—Name and Location

- Dates
- Specialized study program description

Work Experience and Accomplishments (including summer work and internships)

Name of Company or Organization—City, State   From-to-Date
Title and/or specific role

- Describe your responsibilities and what you accomplished in three bullets of one line each
- Use active voice, not passive
- Stay away from jargon and meaningless words

Name of Company or Organization—City, State   From-to-Date
Title and/or specific role

- Describe your responsibilities and what you accomplished in three bullets of one line each
- Use active voice, not passive
- Stay away from jargon and meaningless words

Name of Company or Organization—City, State   From-to-Date
Title and/or specific role

- Describe your responsibilities and what you accomplished in three bullets of one line each
- Use active voice, not passive
- Stay away from jargon and meaningless words

Leadership/Awards/Activities/Special Interests/Volunteer Community Service

- One sentence description of each
- One sentence description of each

First, Middle Initial and Last Name
LinkedIn

Email Address | Cell Phone |

College/University Address	Home Address
Street, City, State Zip	Street, City, State Zip

Career Goal | Career Strengths: This is a focused paragraph of no more than three powerful, personal sentences that capture:

- Your motivation to focus on a particular career or job—your passion
- Education, training, work experience, internships, or unique interests that led you in this direction
- Importance of the work/career

Skills | Areas of Excellence:

1. Life/work/hunger skills
2. Specialized interests
3. Leadership
4. Accomplishments/experience from work or internships

5. Language fluency
6. Work strengths
7. Teamwork experience
8. Key words that address specific job skills noted in a particular posting

---

Education

Bachelor of Arts/Sciences—Specific Degree Title
College or University Name—City, State—Dates of attendance and expected graduation month/year

- GPA: 0.00 / 4.0
- Dean's list/academic honors/teaching or research assistantship/varsity sports teams/awards

Special Studies—Name and Location

- Dates
- Specialized study program description

Work Experience and Accomplishments (including summer work and internships)

From-to-Date **Name of Company or Organization—City, State**
Title and/or specific role

- Describe your responsibilities and what you accomplished in three bullets of one line each
- Use active voice, not passive
- Stay away from jargon and meaningless words

From-to-Date **Name of Company or Organization—City, State**
Title and/or specific role

- Describe your responsibilities and what you accomplished in three bullets of one line each
- Use active voice, not passive
- Stay away from jargon and meaningless words

From-to-Date **Name of Company or Organization—City, State**
Title and/or specific role

- Describe your responsibilities and what you accomplished in three bullets of one line each
- Use active voice, not passive
- Stay away from jargon and meaningless words

Leadership/Awards/Activities/Special Interests/Volunteer Community Service

- One sentence description of each
- One sentence description of each

132

First, Middle Initial and Last Name
Email Address | Cell Phone | LinkedIn

College/University Address
Street, City, State Zip

Home Address
Street, City, State Zip

Career Goal | Career Strengths: This is a focused paragraph of no more than three powerful, personal sentences that capture:

- Your motivation to focus on a particular career or job—your passion
- Education, training, work experience, internships, or unique interests that led you in this direction
- Importance of the work/career

Skills | Areas of Excellence:

- Life/work/hunger skills
- Specialized interests
- Leadership
- Accomplishments/experience from work or internships

- Language fluency
- Work strengths
- Teamwork experience
- Key words that address specific job skills noted in a particular posting

---

Education

College or University Name—City, State
Bachelor of Arts/Sciences—Specific Degree Title—Dates of attendance and expected graduation
- GPA: 0.00 / 4.0
- Dean's list/academic honors/teaching or research assistantship/varsity sports teams/awards

Special Studies – Name and Location
- Dates
- Specialized study program description

Work Experience and Accomplishments (including summer work and internships)

Name of Company or Organization – City, State   From-to-Date
Title and/or specific role
- Describe your responsibilities and what you accomplished in three bullets of one line each
- Use active voice, not passive
- Stay away from jargon and meaningless words

Name of Company or Organization – City, State   From-to-Date
Title and/or specific role
- Describe your responsibilities and what you accomplished in three bullets of one line each
- Use active voice, not passive
- Stay away from jargon and meaningless words

Name of Company or Organization – City, State   From-to-Date
Title and/or specific role
- Describe your responsibilities and what you accomplished in three bullets of one line each
- Use active voice, not passive
- Stay away from jargon and meaningless words

Leadership/Awards/Activities/Special Interests/Volunteer Community Service
- One sentence description of each
- One sentence description of each

APPENDIX TWO

JOB SEARCH WITH LINKEDIN

While new digital technology emerges every day and the job search process becomes ever more dependent on artificial intelligence—especially for entry level opportunities—LinkedIn holds the top spot when it comes to online job search.

It is the largest single source for online job postings, career guidance, employment opportunities and the ability to click "apply" and have your candidacy in front of a recruiter.

Moreover, it is user friendly.

But, as in every aspect of job search, you need to be prepared.

Get your resume together. And if you haven't already, set up your profile. Make sure your LinkedIn page is up and running. Post your resume so that any potential employer can get a quick glance.

Once you're on LinkedIn, become an active participant: connect with others, invite others to connect with you and post news, information and thoughts that help underscore your perspective on issues that you believe are important to your career direction. An active profile gives others insights about you, especially those who may be looking to hire.

And LinkedIn has a job alert option. Depending on your career goals, it can send daily or weekly alerts about jobs and can even tailor them to a particular geographical region, depending on your preferences.

So here is what you should do to take advantage of LinkedIn and today's digital world:

- Start by keeping LinkedIn open on your desktop or mobile. If you have logged out, log in again.

- Review your notifications.

- Click the *Jobs* option at the top of the page.

- You'll see a header that says: *our dream job's just a search away ...*".

- On the left-hand side, you will see *Search jobs,* along with some *Suggested job searches* which, thanks to technology have already been culled from your resume or other background information you've posted on LinkedIn.

- If any of those suggestions match your goals, click *Search* and you're off and running. If not, add your own.

- To narrow down your search, on the right-hand side you'll also see the prompt *Geographic area,* already identified. Again, technology has drawn on your posted materials to fill in that category. But, change it. You may want to move somewhere else.

- On the far right-hand side, you will see the button to *Search.* When you are ready, click.

- A new page will open and you'll have a host of *Results* to look at. It might be only a few dozen or thousands. It all depends on real-time job postings and your qualifications.

- On that same page, you will see a button labeled *Job Alert*. Click on that, it will open a new window that gives you the opportunity to select how often (daily or weekly) and by email or notification you wish to receive job notices.

This is technology at its best. You can get emails daily for potential jobs. You can then click through the email and look at the job posting itself.

LinkedIn gives you an advantage.

Make the most of it.

Jobs aren't just going to be handed to you on your lap.

NOTES

Made in the USA
Columbia, SC
09 March 2021